Esmerelda

Frances Hodgson Burnett

Table of Contents

Esmerelda

Frances Hodgson Burnett

To begin, I am a Frenchman, a teacher of languages and a poor man; — necessarily a poor man, as the great world would say, or I should not be a teacher of languages and my wife a copyist of great pictures, selling her copies at small prices. In our own eyes, it is true, we are not so poor — my Clelie and I. Looking back upon our past we congratulate ourselves upon our prosperous condition. There was a time when we were poorer than we are now, and were not together, and were, moreover, in London instead of in Paris. These were indeed calamities: to be poor, to teach, to live apart, not even knowing each other — and in England! In England we spent years; we instructed imbeciles of all grades; we were chilled by east winds, and tortured by influenza; we vainly strove to conciliate the appalling English; we were discouraged and desolate. But this, thank lebon Dieu! is past. We are united; we have our little apartment — upon the fifth floor, it is true, but still not hopelessly far from the Champs Elysees. Clelie paints her little pictures, or copies those of some greater artist, and finds sale for them. She is not a great artist herself, and is charmingly conscious of the fact.

"At fifteen," she says, "I regretted that I was not a genius; at five and twenty, I rejoice that I made the discovery so early, and so gave myself time to become grateful for the small gifts bestowed upon me. Why should I eat out my heart with envy? Is it not possible that I might be a less clever woman than I am, and a less lucky one?"

Esmerelda

On my part I have my pupils, — French pupils who take lessons in English, German, or Italian; English or American pupils who generally learn French, and, upon the whole, I do not suffer from lack of patrons.

It is my habit when Clelie is at work upon a copy in one of the great galleries to accompany her to the scene of her labor in the morning and call for her at noon, and, in accordance with this habit, I made my way to the Louvre at midday upon one occasion three years ago.

I found my wife busy at her easel in the Grande Galerie, and when I approached her and laid my hand upon her shoulder, as was my wont, she looked up with a smile and spoke to me in a cautious undertone.

"I am glad," she said, "that you are not ten minutes later. Look at those extraordinary people."

She still leaned back in her chair and looked up at me, but made, at the same time, one of those indescribable movements of the head which a clever woman can render so significant.

This slight gesture directed me at once to the extraordinary people to whom she referred.

"Are they not truly wonderful?" she asked.

There were two of them, evidently father and daughter, and they sat side by side upon a seat placed in an archway, and regarded hopelessly one of the finest works in the gallery. The father was a person undersized and elderly. His face was tanned and seamed, as if with years of rough out–door labor; the effect produced upon him by his clothes was plainly one of actual suffering, both physical and mental. His stiff hands refused to meet the efforts of his gloves to fit them; his body shrank from his garments; if he had not been pathetic, he would have been ridiculous. But he was pathetic. It was evident that he was not so attired of his own free will, that only a patient nature, inured by long custom to discomfort, sustained him, — that he was in the gallery under protest, — that he did not understand the paintings, and that they perplexed — overwhelmed him.

Esmerelda

The daughter it is almost impossible to describe, and yet I must attempt to describe her. She had a slender and pretty figure; there were slight marks of the sun on her face also, and, as in her father's case, the richness of her dress was set at defiance by a strong element of incongruousness. She had black hair and gray eyes, and she sat with folded hands staring at the picture before her in dumb uninterestedness.

Clelie had taken up her brush again, and was touching up her work here and there.

"They have been here two hours," she said. "They are waiting for some one. At first they tried to look about them as others did. They wandered from seat to seat, and sat down, and looked as you see them doing now. What do you think of them? To what nation should you ascribe them?"

"They are not French," I answered. "And they are not English."

"If she was English," said Clelie, "the girl would be more conscious of herself, and of what we might possibly be saying. She is only conscious that she is out of place and miserable. She does not care for us at all. I have never seen Americans like them before, but I am convinced that they are Americans."

She laid aside her working materials and proceeded to draw on her gloves.

"We will go and look at that `Tentation de St. Antoine' of Teniers," she said,"and we may hear them speak. I confess I am devoured by an anxiety to hear them speak."

Accordingly, a few moments later an amiable young couple stood before "La Tentation," regarding it with absorbed and critical glances.

But the father and daughter did not seem to see us. They looked disconsolately about them, or at the picture before which they sat. Finally, however, we were rewarded by hearing them speak to each other. The father addressed the young lady slowly and deliberately, and with an accent which, but for my long residence in England and familiarity with some forms of its patois, I should find it impossible to transcribe.

"Esmeraldy," he said, "your ma's a long time a−comin'."

3

Esmerelda

"Yes," answered the girl, with the same accent, and in a voice wholly listless and melancholy, "she's a long time."

Clelie favored me with one of her rapid side glances. The study of character is her grand passion, and her special weakness is a fancy for the singular and incongruous. I have seen her stand in silence, and regard with positive interest one of her former patronesses who was overwhelming her with contumelious violence, seeming entirely un-conscious of all else but that the woman was of a species novel to her, and therefore worthy of delicate observation.

"It is as I said," she whispered. "They are Americans, but of an order entirely new."

Almost the next instant she touched my arm.

"Here is the mother!" she exclaimed. "She is coming this way. See!"

A woman advanced rapidly toward our part of the gallery, — a small, angry woman, with an ungraceful figure, and a keen brown eye. She began to speak aloud while still several feet distant from the waiting couple.

"Come along," she said. "I've found a place at last, though I've been all the morning at it, — and the woman who keeps the door speaks English."

"They call 'em," remarked the husband, meekly rising, "con-ser-ges. I wonder why."

The girl rose also, still with her hopeless, abstracted air, and followed the mother, who led the way to the door. Seeing her move forward, my wife uttered an admiring exclamation.

"She is more beautiful than I thought," she said. "She holds herself marvelously. She moves with the freedom of some fine wild creature."

And, as the party disappeared from view, her regret at losing them drew from her a sigh. She discussed them with characteristic enthusiasm all the way home. She even concocted a very probable little romance. One would always imagine so many things concerning Americans. They were so extraordinary a people; they acquired wealth by such peculiar

4

means; their country was so immense; their resources were so remarkable. These persons, for instance, were plainly persons of wealth, and as plainly had risen from the people. The mother was not quite so wholly untaught as the other two, but she was more objectionable.

"One can bear with the large simplicity of utter ignorance," said my fairphilosopher. "One frequently finds it gentle and unworldly, but the other is odious because it is always aggressive and narrow."

She had taken a strong feminine dislike to Madame la Mere.

"She makes her family miserable," she said. "She drags them from place to place. Possibly there is a lover, — more possibly than not. The girl's eyes wore a peculiar look, — as if they searched for something far away."

She had scarcely concluded her charming little harangue when we reached our destination; but, as we passed through the entrance, she paused to speak to the curly-headed child of the concierge whose mother held him by the hand.

"We shall have new arrivals to-morrow," said the good woman, who was always ready for friendly gossip. "The apartment upon the first floor," and she nodded to me significantly, and with good-natured encouragement. "Perhaps you may get pupils," she added. "They are Americans, and speak only English, and there is a young lady, Madame says."

"Americans!" exclaimed Clelie, with sudden interest.

"Americans," answered the concierge. "It was Madame who came. Mon Dieu! if was wonderful! So rich and so — so — — "filling up the blank by ashrug of deep meaning.

"It cannot have been long since they were — peasants," her voice dropping into a cautious whisper.

"Why not our friends of the Louvre?" said Clelie as we went on upstairs.

"Why not?" I replied. "It is very possible."

5

Esmerelda

The next day there arrived at the house numberless trunks of large dimensions, superintended by the small angry woman and a maid. An hour later came a carriage, from whose door emerged the young lady and her father. Both looked pale and fagged; both were led upstairs in the midst of voluble comments and commands by the mother; and both, entering the apartment, seemed swallowed up by it, as we saw and heard nothing further of them. Clelie was indignant.

"It is plain that the mother overwhelms them," she said. "A girl of that age should speak and be interested in any novelty. This one would be if she were not wretched. And the poor little husband — — !"

"My dear," I remarked, "you are a feminine Bayard. You engage yourself with such ardor in everybody's wrongs."

When I returned from my afternoon's work a few days later, I found Clelie again excited. She had been summoned to the first floor by Madame.

"I went into the room," said Clelie, "and found the mother and daughter together. Mademoiselle, who stood by the fire, had evidently been weeping. Madame was in an abrupt and angry mood. She wasted no words. `I want you to give her lessons,' she said, making an ungraceful gesture in the direction of her daughter. `What do you charge a lesson?' And on my telling her, she engaged me at once. `It's a great deal, but I guess I can pay as well as other people,' she remarked."

A few of the lessons were given downstairs, and then Clelie preferred a request to Madame.

"If you will permit Mademoiselle to come to my room, you will confer a favor upon me," she said.

Fortunately, her request was granted, and so I used afterward to come home and find Mademoiselle Esmeralda in our little salon at work disconsolately and tremulously. She found it difficult to hold her pencil in the correct manner, and one morning she let it drop, and burst into tears.

Esmerelda

"Don't you see I shall never do it!" she answered, miserably. "Don't you see Icouldn't, even if my heart was in it, and it aint at all!"

She held out her little hands piteously for Clelie to look at. They were well enough shaped, and would have been pretty if they had not been robbed of their youthful suppleness by labor.

"I've been used to work," she said, "rough work all my life, and my hands aint like yours."

"But you must not be discouraged, Mademoiselle," said Clelie gently. "Time — — "

"Time," interposed the girl, with a frightened look in her pretty gray eyes. "That's what I can't bear to think of — the time that's to come."

This was the first of many outbursts of confidence. Afterward she related to Clelie, with the greatest naivete, the whole history of the family affairs.

They had been the possessors of some barren mountain lands in North Carolina, and her description of their former life was wonderful indeed to the ears of the Parisian. She herself had been brought up with marvelous simplicity and hardihood, barely learning to read and write, and in absolute ignorance of society. A year ago iron had been discovered upon their property, and the result had been wealth and misery for father and daughter. The mother, who had some vague fancies of the attractions of the great outside world, was ambitious and restless. Monsieur, who was a mild and accommodating person, could only give way before her stronger will.

"She always had her way with us," said Mademoiselle Esmeralda, scratching nervously upon the paper before her with her pencil, at this part of the relation. "We did not want to leave home, neither me nor father, and father said more than I ever heard him say before at one time. `Mother,' says he, `let me an' Esmeraldy stay at home, an' you go an' enjoy your tower. You've had more schoolin', an' you'll be more at home than we should. You're useder to city ways, havin' lived in `Lizabethville.' But it only vexed her. People in town had been talking to her about traveling and letting me learn things, and she'd set her mind on it."

7

Esmerelda

She was very simple and unsophisticated. To the memory of her former truly singular life she clung with unshaken fidelity. She recurred to it constantly. The novelty and luxury of her new existence seemed to have no attractions for her. One thing even my Clelie found incomprehensible, while she fancied she understood the rest — she did not appear to be moved to pleasure even by our beloved Paris.

"It is a true maladie du pays," Clelie remarked to me. "And that is not all."

Nor was it all. One day the whole truth was told amid a flood of tears.

"I — I was going to be married," cried the poor child. "I was to have been mar−ried the week the ore was found. I was — all ready, and mother — mother shut right down on us."

Clelie glanced at me in amazed questioning.

"It is a kind of argot which belongs only to Americans," I answered in an undertone. "The alliance was broken off."

"Ciel!" exclaimed my Clelie between her small shut teeth. "The woman is a fiend!"

She was wholly absorbed in her study of this unworldly and untaught nature. She was full of sympathy for its trials and tenderness, and for its pain. Even the girl's peculiarities of speech were full of interest to her. She made serious and intelligent efforts to understand them, as if she studied a new language.

"It is not common argot," she said. `It has its subtleties. One continually finds somewhere an original idea — sometimes even a bonmot, which startles one by its pointedness. As you say, however, it belongs only to the Americans and their remarkable country. A French mind can only arrive at its climaxes through a grave and occasionally tedious research, which would weary most persons, but which, however, does not weary me."

The confidence of Mademoiselle Esmeralda was easily won. She became attached to us both, and particularly to Clelie. When her mother was absent or occupied, she stole upstairs to our apartment and spent with us the moments of leisure chance afforded her. She liked our rooms, she told my wife, because they were small, and our society because

8

we were "clever," which we discovered afterward meant "amiable." But she was always pale and out of spirits. She would sit before our fire silent and abstracted.

"You must not mind if I don't talk," she would say. "I can't; and it seems to help me to get to sit and think about things. Mother wont let me do it down-stairs."

We became also familiar with the father. One day I met him upon the staircase,and to my amazement he stopped as if he wished to address me. I raised my hat and bade him good-morning. On his part he drew forth a large handkerchief and began to rub the palms of his hands with awkward timidity.

"How-dy?" he said.

I confess that at the moment I was covered with confusion. I who was a teacher of English and flattered myself that I wrote and spoke it fluently, did not understand. Immediately, however, it flashed across my mind that the word was a species of salutation. (Which I finally discovered to be the case.) I bowed again and thanked him, hazarding the reply that my health was excellent, and an inquiry as to the state of Madame's. He rubbed his hands still more nervously, and answered me in the slow and deliberate manner I had observed at the Louvre.

"Thank ye," he said, "she's doin' tol'able well, is mother — as well as common. And she's a-enjoyin' herself, too. I wish we was all — — "

But there he checked himself and glanced hastily about him. Then he began again, —

"Esmeraldy," he said, — "Esmeraldy thinks a heap on you. She takes a sight of comfort out of Mis' Des — — I can't call your name, but I mean your wife."

"Madame Desmarres," I replied, "is rejoiced indeed to have won the friendship of Mademoiselle."

"Yes," he proceeded, "she takes a sight of comfort in you ans all. An' she needs comfort, does Esmeraldy."

Esmerelda

There ensued a slight pause which somewhat embarrassed me, for at every pause he regarded me with an air of meek and hesitant appeal.

"She's a little down–sperrited is Esmeraldy," he said. "An'," adding this suddenly in a subdued and fearful tone, "so am I."

Having said this he seemed to feel that he had overstepped a barrier. He seized the lapel of my coat and held me prisoner, pouring forth his confessions with a faith in my interest by which I was at once amazed and touched.

"You see it's this way," he said, — " it's this way, Mister. We're home folks, me an' Esmeraldy, an' we're a long way from home, an' it sorter seems like we didn't get no useder to it than we was at first. We're not like mother. Mother she was raised in a town, — she was raised in 'Lizabethville, — an' she allers took to town ways; but me an'Esmeraldy, we was raised in the mountains, right under the shadder of old Bald, an' town goes hard with us. Seems like we're allers a thinkin' of North Callina. An' mother she gits outed, which is likely. She says we'd ought to fit ourselves fur our higher spear, an' I dessay we'd ought, — but you see it goes sorter hard with us. An' Esmeraldy she has her trouble an' I can't help a sympathizin' with her, fur young folks will be young folks; an' I was young folks once myself. Once — once I sot a heap o' store by mother. So you see how it is."

"It is very sad, Monsieur," I answered with gravity. Singular as it may appear, this was not so laughable to me as it might seem. It was so apparent that he did not anticipate ridicule. And my Clelie's interest in these people also rendered them sacred in my eyes.

"Yes," he returned, "that's so; an' sometimes it's wuss than you'd think — when mother's outed. An' that's why I'm glad as Mis' Dimar an' Esmeraldy is such friends."

It struck me at this moment that he had some request to make of me. He grasped the lapel of my coat somewhat more tightly as if requiring additional support, and finally bent forward and addressed me with caution, "Do you think as Mis' Dimar would mind it ef now an' then I has to step in fur Esmeraldy, an' set a little — just in a kinder neigh–borin' way. Esmeraldy, she says you're so sosherble. And I haint been sosherble with no one fur — fur a right smart spell. And it seems like I kinder hanker arter it. You've no idea, Mister, how lonesome a man can git when he hankers to be sosherble an' haint no one to be sosherble with. Mother, she says, `Go out on the Champs Elizy and promenard,' and I've done it; but some ways it don't reach the spot. I don't seem to get sosherble with no one I've spoke to — may be through us speakin' different languages, an' not comin' to a understandin'. I've tried it loud an' I've tried it low an' encouragen', but someways we never seemed to get on. An' ef Mis' Dimar wouldn't take no exceptions at mea-droppin' in, I feel as ef I should be sorter uplifted — if she'd only allow it once a week or even fewer."

"Monsieur," I replied with warmth, "I beg you will consider oursalon at your disposal, not once a week but at all times, and Madame Desmarres would certainly join me in the invitation if she were upon the spot."

He released the lapel of my coat and grasped my hand, shaking it with fervor.

"Now, that's clever, that is," he said. "An' its friendly, an' I'm obligated to ye."

Since he appeared to have nothing further to say we went down-stairs together. At the door we parted.

"I'm a-goin'," he remarked, "to the Champs Elizy to promenard. Where are you a-goin'?"

To the Boulevard Haussmann, Monsieur, to give a lesson," I returned. "I will wish you good-morning."

"Good-mornin'," he answered. "Bong" — reflecting deeply for a moment — "Bong jore. I'm a tryin' to learn it, you see, with a view to bein' more sosherbler. Bong jore." And thus took his departure.

After this we saw him frequently. In fact it became his habit to follow Mademoiselle Esmeralda in all her visits to our apartment. A few minutes after her arrival we usually heard a timid knock upon the outer door, which proved to emanate from Mon-sieur, who always entered with a laborious "Bong jore," and always slipped deprecatingly into the least comfortable chair near the fire, hurriedly concealing his hat beneath it.

In him also my Clelie became much interested. On my own part I could not cease to admire the fine feeling and delicate tact she continually exhibited in her manner toward him. In time he even appeared to lose something of his first embarrassment and discomfort, though he was always inclined to a reverent silence in her presence.

"He don't say much, don't father," said Mademoiselle Esmeralda, with tears in her pretty eyes. "He's like me, but you don't know what comfort he's taking when he sits and listens and stirs his chocolate round and round without drinking it. He doesn't drink it because he aint used to it; but he likes to have it when we do, because he says it makes him feel sosherble. He's trying to learn to drink it too — he practices every day a little at a time. He was powerful afraid at first that you'd take exceptions to him doing nothing but stir it round; but I told him I knew you wouldn't for you wasn't that kind."

"I find him," said Clelie to me, "inexpressibly mournful, — even though he excites one to smiles upon all occasions. Is it not mournful that his very suffering should be absurd. Mon Dieu! he does not wear his clothes — he bears them about with him — he simply carries them."

It was about this time that Mademoiselle Esmeralda was rendered doubly unhappy. Since their residence in Paris Madame had been industriously occupied in making efforts to enter society. She had struggled violently and indefatigably. She was at once persistent and ambitious. She had used every means that lay in her power, and, most of all, she had used her money. Naturally, she had found people upon the outskirts of good circles who would accept her with her money. Consequently, she had obtained acquaintances of a class, and was bold enough to employ them as stepping–stones. At all events, she began to receive invitations, and to discover opportunities to pay visits, and to take her daughter with her. Accordingly, Mademoiselle Esmeralda was placed upon exhibition. She was dressed by experienced artistes. She was forced from her seclusion, and obliged to drive and call, and promenade.

Her condition was pitiable. While all this was torture to her experience and timidity, her fear of her mother rendered her wholly submissive. Each day brought with it some new trial. She was admired for many reasons, — by some for her wealth, of which all had heard rumors; by others for her freshness and beauty. The silence and sensitiveness which arose from shyness, and her ignorance of all social rules, were called naivete and modesty, and people who abhorred her mother, not unfrequently were charmed with her, and consequently Madame found her also an instrument of some consequence.

Esmerelda

In her determination to overcome all obstacles, Madame even condescended to apply to my wife, whose influence over Mademoiselle she was clever enough not to undervalue.

"I want you to talk to Mademoiselle," she said. "She thinks a great deal of you, and I want you to give her some good advice. You know what society is, and you know that she ought to be proud of her advantages, and not make a fool of herself. Many a girl would be glad enough of what she has before her. She's got money, and she's got chances, and I don't begrudge her anything. She can spend all she likes on clothes and things, and I'll take her anywhere if she'll behave herself. They wear me out — her and her father. It's her father that's ruined her, and her living as she's done. Her father never knew anything, and he's made a pet of her, and got her into his way of thinking. It's ridiculous how little ambition they have, and she might marry as well as any girl. There's a marquis that's quite in love with her at this moment, and she's as afraid of him as death, and cries if I even mention him, though he's a nice enough man, if he is a bit elderly. Now, I want you to reason with her."

This Clelie told me afterward.

"And upon going away," she ended, "she turned round toward me, setting her face into an indescribable expression of hardness and obstinacy. `I want her to understand,'she said, `that she's cut off forever from anything that's happened before. There's the Atlantic Ocean and many a mile of land between her and North Carolina, and so she may as well give that up.'"

Two or three days after this Mademoiselle came to our apartment in great grief. She had left Madame in a violent ill–temper. They had received invitations to a ball at which they were to meet the marquis. Madame had been elated, and the discovery of Mademoiselle's misery and trepidation had roused her indignation. There had been a painful scene, and Mademoiselle had been overwhelmed as usual.

She knelt before the fire and wept despairingly.

"I'd rather die than go," she said. "I can't stand it. I can't get used to it. The light, and the noise, and the talk, hurts me, and I don't know what I am doing. And people stare at me, and I make mistakes, and I'm not fit for it — and — and — I'd rather be dead fifty thousand times than let that man come near me. I hate him, and I'm afraid of him, and I wish I was dead."

At this juncture came the timid summons upon the door, and the father entered with a disturbed and subdued air. He did not conceal his hat, but held it in his hands, and turned it round and round in an agitated manner as he seated himself beside his daughter.

"Esmeraldy," he said, "don't you take it so hard, honey. Mother, she's kinder outed, an' she's not at herself rightly. Don't you never mind. Mother she means well, but — but she's got a sorter curious way of showin' it. She's got a high sperrit, an' we'd ought to 'low fur it, and not take it so much to heart. Mis' Dimar here knows how high–sperrited people is sometimes, I dessay, — an' mother she's got a powerful high sperrit."

But the poor child only wept more hopelessly. It was not only the cruelty of her mother which oppressed her, it was the wound she bore in her heart.

Clelie's eyes filled with tears as she regarded her.

The father was also more broken in spirit than he wished it to appear. His weather–beaten face assumed an expression of deep melancholy which at last betrayed itself in an evidently inadvertent speech.

"I wish — I wish," he faltered. "Lord! I'd give a heap to see Wash now. I'd give a heap to see him, Esmeraldy."

It was as if the words were the last straw. The girl turned toward him and flung herself upon his breast with a passionate cry.

"Oh, father!" she sobbed, "we sha'n't never see him again — never — never! nor the mountains, nor the people that cared for us. We've lost it all, and we can't get it back, — and we haven't a soul that's near to us, — and we're all alone, — you and me, father, and Wash. Wash, he thinks we don't care."

I must confess to a momentary spasm of alarm, her grief was so wild and overwhelming. One hand was flung about her father's neck, and the other pressed itself against her side, as if her heart was breaking.

Esmerelda

Clelie bent down and lifted her up, consoling her tenderly.

"Mademoiselle," she said, "do not despair. Le Bon Dieu will surely have pity."

The father drew forth the large linen handkerchief, and, unfolding it slowly, applied it to his eyes.

"Yes, Esmeraldy," he said; "don't let us give out, — at least don't you give out. It doesn't matter fur me, Esmeraldy, because, you see, I must hold on to mother, as I swore not to go back on; but you're young an' likely, Esmeraldy, an' don't you give out yet, fur the Lord's sake."

But she did not cease weeping until she had wholly fatigued herself, and by this time there arrived a message from Madame, who required her presence down–stairs. Monsieur was somewhat alarmed, and rose precipitately, but Mademoiselle was too full of despair to admit of fear.

"It's only the dress–maker," she said. "You can stay where you are, father, and she wont guess we've been together, and it'll be better for us both."

And accordingly she obeyed the summons alone.

Great were the preparations made by Madame for the entertainment. My wife,to whom she displayed the costumes and jewels she had purchased, was aroused to an admiration truly feminine.

She had had the discretion to trust to the taste of the artistes, and had restrained them in nothing. Consequently, all that was to be desired in the appearance of Mademoiselle Esmeralda upon the eventful evening was happiness. With her mother's permission, she came to our room to display herself, Monsieur following her with an air of awe and admiration commingled. Her costume was rich and exquisite, and her beauty beyond criticism; but as she stood in the center of our little salon to be looked at,she presented an appearance to move one's heart. The pretty young face which had by this time lost its slight traces of the sun had also lost some of its bloom; the slight figure was not so round nor so erect as it had been, and moved with less of spirit and girlishness.

15

Esmerelda

It appeared that Monsieur observed this also, for he stood apart regarding her with evident depression, and occasionally used his handkerchief with a violence that was evidently meant to conceal some secret emotion.

"You're not so peart as you was, Esmeraldy," he remarked, tremulously; "not as peart by a right smart, and what with that, and what with your fixin's, Wash — I mean the home—folks," hastily — "they'd hardly know ye."

He followed her down—stairs mournfully when she took her departure, and Clelie and myself being left alone interested ourselves in various speculations concerning them, as was our habit.

"This Monsieur Wash," remarked Clelie, "is clearly the lover. Poor child! how passionately she regrets him, — and thousands of miles lie between them — thousands of miles!"

It was not long after this that, on my way down—stairs to make a trifling purchase, I met with something approaching an adventure. It so chanced that, as I descended the staircase of the second floor, the door of the first floor apartment was thrown open, and from it issued Mademoiselle Esmeralda and her mother on their way to their waiting carriage. My interest in the appearance of Mademoiselle in her white robes and sparkling jewels so absorbed me that I inadvertently brushed against a figure which stood in the shadow regarding them also. Turning at once to apologize, I found myself confronting a young man, — tall, powerful, but with a sad and haggard face, and attired in a strange and homely dress which had a foreign look.

"Monsieur!" I exclaimed, "a thousand pardons. I was so unlucky as not to see you."

But he did not seem to hear. He remained silent, gazing fixedly at the ladies until they had disappeared, and then, on my addressing him again, he awakened, as it were, with a start.

"It doesn't matter," he answered, in a heavy bewildered voice and in English, and turning back made his way slowly up the stairs.

Esmerelda

But even the utterance of this brief sentence had betrayed to my practiced ear a peculiar accent — an accent which, strange to say, bore a likeness to that of our friends down–stairs, and which caused me to stop a moment at the lodge of theconcierge, and ask her a question or so.

"Have we a new occupant upon the fifth floor?" I inquired."A person who speaks English?"

She answered me with a dubious expression.

You must mean the strange young man upon the sixth," she said. "He is a new one and speaks English. Indeed, he does not speak anything else, or even understand a word. Mon Dieu! the trials one encounters with such persons, — endeavoring to comprehend, poor creatures, and failing always, — and this one is worse than the rest and looks more wretched — as if he had not a friend in the world."

"What is his name?" I asked.

"How can one remember their names? — it is worse than impossible. This one is frightful. But he has no letters, thank Heaven. If there should arrive one with an impossible name upon it, I should take it to him and run the risk."

Naturally, Clelie, to whom I related the incident, was much interested. But it was some time before either of us saw the hero of it again, though both of us confessed to having been upon the watch for him. The conciergecould only tell us that he lived a secluded life — rarely leaving his room in the day–time, and seeming to be very poor.

"He does not work and eats next to nothing," she said. "Late at night he occasionally carries up a loaf, and once he treated himself to a cup of bouillon from the restaurant at the corner — but it was only once, poor young man. He is at least very gentle and well–conducted."

So it was not to be wondered at that we did not see him. Clelie mentioned him to her young friend, but Mademoiselle's interest in him was only faint and ephemeral. She had not the spirit to rouse herself to any strong emotion.

Esmerelda

"I dare say he's an American," she said.

There are plenty of Americans in Paris, but none of them seem a bit nearer to me than if they were French. They are all rich and fine, and they all like the life here better than the life at home. This is the first poor one I have heard of."

Each day brought fresh unhappiness to her. Madame was inexorable. She spent a fortune upon toilette for her, and insisted upon dragging her from place to place, and wearying her with gayeties from which her sad young heart shrank. Each afternoon their equipage was to be seen upon the Champs Elysees, and each evening it stood before the door waiting to bear them to some place of festivity.

Mademoiselle's bete noir, the marquis, who was a debilitated roue in search of a fortune, attached himself to them upon all occasions.

"Bah!" said Clelie with contempt, "she amazes one by her imbecility — this woman. Truly, one would imagine that her vulgar sharpness would teach her that his objectis to use her as a tool, and that having gained Mademoiselle's fortune, he will treat them with brutality and derision."

But she did not seem to see — possibly she fancied that having obtained him for a son–in–law, she would be bold and clever enough to outwit and control him. Consequently, he was encouraged and fawned upon, and Mademoiselle grew thin and pale and large–eyed, and wore continually an expression of secret terror.

Only in her visits to our fifth floor did she dare to give way to her grief, and truly at such times both my Clelie and I were greatly affected. Upon one occasion indeed she filled us both with alarm.

"Do you know what I shall do?" she said, stopping suddenly in the midst of her weeping. "I'll bear it as long as I can, and then I'll put an end to it. There's — there's always the Seine left, and I've laid awake and thought of it many a night. Father and me saw a man taken out of it one day, and the people said he was a Tyrolean and drowned himself because he was so poor and lonely — and — and so far from home."

Esmerelda

Upon the very morning she made this speech I saw again our friend of the sixth floor. In going down–stairs I came upon him, sitting upon one of the steps as if exhausted, and when he turned his face upward, its pallor and haggardness startled me. His tall form was wasted, his eyes were hollow, the peculiarities I had before observed were doubly marked — he was even emaciated.

"Monsieur," I said in English, "you appear indisposed. You have been ill. Allow me to assist you to your room."

"No, thank you," he answered. "It's only weakness. I — I sorter give out. Don't trouble yourself. I shall get over it directly."

Something in his face which was a very young and well–looking one, forced me to leave him in silence, merely bowing as I did so. I felt instinctively that to remain would be to give him additional pain.

As I passed the room of the concierge, however, the excellent woman beckoned to me to approach her.

"Did you see the young man?" she inquired rather anxiously. "He has shown himself this morning for the first time in three days. There is something wrong. It is my impression that he suffers want — that he is starving himself to death!"

Her rosy countenance absolutely paled as she uttered these last words, retreating a pace from me, and touching my arm with her fore–finger.

"He has carried up even less bread than usual during the last few weeks," she added "and there has been no bouillon whatever. A young man cannot live only on dry bread, and too little of that. He will perish; and apart from the inhumanity of the thing, it will be unpleasant for the other locataires."

I wasted no time in returning to Clelie, having indeed some hope that I might find the poor fellow still occupying his former position upon the staircase. But in this I met with disappointment: he was gone and I could only relate to my wife what I had heard, and trust to her discretion. As I had expected, she was deeply moved.

Esmerelda

"It is terrible," she said. "And it is also a delicate and difficult matter to manage. But what can one do? There is only one thing — I who am a woman, and have suffered privation myself, may venture."

Accordingly, she took her departure for the floor above. I heard her light summons upon the door of one of the rooms, but heard no reply. At last, however, the door was opened gently, and with a hesitance that led me to imagine that it was Clelie herself who had pushed it open, and immediately afterward I was sure that she uttered an alarmed exclamation. I stepped out upon the landing and called to her in a subdued tone —

"Clelie," I said, "did I hear you speak?"

"Yes," she returned from within the room. "Come at once, and bring with you some brandy."

In the shortest possible time I had joined her in the room, which was bare, cold and unfurnished — a mere garret, in fact, containing nothing but a miserable bedstead. Upon the floor near the window knelt Clelie, supporting with her knee and arm the figure of the young man she had come to visit.

"Quick with the brandy," she exclaimed. "This may be a faint, but it looks like death." She had found the door partially open, and receiving no answer to her knock, had pushed it farther ajar and caught a glimpse of the fallen figure, and hurried to its assistance.

To be as brief as possible, — we both remained at the young man's side during the whole of the night. As the concierge had said, he was perishing from inanition, and the physician we called in assured us that only the most constant attention would save his life.

"Monsieur," Clelie explained to him upon the first occasion upon which heopened his eyes. "You are ill and alone, and we wish to befriend you." And he was too weak to require from her anything more definite.

Physically he was a person to admire. In health his muscular power must have been immense. He possessed the frame of a young giant, and yet there was in his face alook of innocence and inexperience amazing even when one recollected his youth.

Esmerelda

"It is the look," said Clelie, regarding him attentively, — "the look one sees in the faces of Monsieur and his daughter down-stairs; the look of a person who has lived a simple life, and who knows absolutely nothing of the world."

It is possible that this may have prepared the reader for thedenoument which followed; but singular as it may appear, it did not prepare either Clelie or myself — perhaps because we had seen the world, and having learned to view it in a practical light, were not prepared to encounter suddenly a romance almost unparalleled.

The next morning I was compelled to go out to give my lessons as usual, and left Clelie with our patient. On my return, my wife, hearing my footsteps, came out and met me upon the landing. She was moved by the strongest emotion and much excited her cheeks were pale and her eyes shone.

"Do not go in yet," she said, "I have something to tell you. It is almost incredible; but — but it is — the lover!"

For a moment we remained silent — standing looking at each other. To me it seemed incredible indeed.

"He could not give her up," Clelie went on, "until he was sure she wished to discard him. The mother had employed all her ingenuity to force him to believe that such was the case, but he could not rest until he had seen his betrothed face to face. So he followed her, — poor, inexperienced and miserable, — and when at last he saw her at a distance, the luxury with which she was surrounded caused his heart to fail him, and be gave way to despair."

I accompanied her into the room, and heard the rest from his own lips. He gathered together all his small savings, and made his journey in the cheapest possible way, — in the steerage of the vessel, and in third-class carriages, — so that he might have some trifle left to subsist upon.

"I've a little farm," he said, "and there's a house on it, but I wouldn't sell that. If she cared to go, it was all I had to take her to, an' I'd worked hard to buy it. I'd worked hard, early and late, always thinking that some day we'd begin life there together — Esmeraldy and me."

Esmerelda

"Since neither sea, nor land, nor cruelty, could separate them," said Clelie to me during the day, "it is not I who will help to hold them apart."

So when Mademoiselle came for her lesson that afternoon, it was Clelie's task to break the news to her, — to tell her that neither sea nor land lay between herself and her lover, and that he was faithful still.

She received the information as she might have received a blow, — staggering backward, and whitening, and losing her breath; but almost immediately afterward she uttered a sad cry of disbelief and anguish.

"No, no," she said, "it — it isn't true! I wont believe it — I mustn't. There's half the world between us. Oh! don't try to make me believe it, — when it can't be true!"

"Come with me," replied Clelie.

Never — never in my life has it been my fate to see, before or since, a sight so touching as the meeting of these two young hearts. When the door of the cold, bare room opened, and Mademoiselle Esmeralda entered, the lover held out his weak arms with a sob, — a sob of rapture, and yet terrible to hear.

"I thought you'd gone back on me, Esmeraldy," he cried. "I thought you'd gone back on me."

Clelie and I turned away and left them as the girl fell upon her knees at his side.

The effect produced upon the father — who had followed Mademoiselle as usual, and whom we found patiently seated upon the bottom step of the flight of stairs, awaiting our arrival — was almost indescribable.

He sank back upon his seat with a gasp, clutching at his hat with both hands. He also disbelieved.

"Wash!" he exclaimed weakly. "Lord! no! Lord! no! Not Wash! Wash, he's in North Callina. Lord! no!"

Esmerelda

He is upstairs," returned Clelie, "and Mademoiselle is with him."

During the recovery of the Monsieur Wash, though but little was said upon the subject, it is my opinion that the minds of each of our number pointed only toward one course in the future.

In Mademoiselle's demeanor there appeared a certain air of new courage and determination, though she was still pallid and anxious. It was as if she had passed a climax and had gained strength. Monsieur, the father, was alternately nervous and dejected, or in feverishly high spirits. Occasionally he sat for some time without speaking, merely gazing into the fire with a hand upon each knee; and it was one evening, after a more than usually prolonged silence of this description, that he finally took upon himself the burden which lay upon us unitedly.

"Esmeraldy," he remarked, tremulously, and with manifest trepidation, — "Esme–raldy, I've been thinkin' — it's time — we broke it to mother."

The girl lost color, but she lifted her head steadily.

"Yes, father," she answered, "it's time."

"Yes," he echoed, rubbing his knees slowly, "it's time; an', Esmeraldy, it's a thing to — to sorter set a man back."

"Yes, father," she answered again.

"Yes," as before, though his voice broke somewhat; "an' I dessay you know how it'll be, Esmeraldy, — that you'll have to choose between mother and Wash."

She sat by her lover, and for answer she dropped her face upon his hand with a sob.

"An' — an' you've chose Wash, Esmeraldy?"

"Yes, father."

He hesitated a moment, and then took his hat from its place of concealment and rose.

Esmerelda

"It's nat'ral," he said, "an' it's right. I wouldn't want it no other way. An' you mustn't mind, Esmeraldy, it's bein' kinder rough on me, as can't go back on mother, havin' swore to cherish her till death do us part. You've allus been a good gal to me, an' we've thought a heap on each other, an' I reckon it can allus be the same way, even though we're sep'rated, fur it's nat'ral you should have chose Wash, an' — an' I wouldn't have it no other way, Esmeraldy. Now I'll go an' have it out with mother."

We were all sufficiently unprepared for the announcement to be startled by it. Mademoiselle Esmeralda, who was weeping bitterly, half sprang to her feet.

"To—night!" she said. "Oh! father!"

"Yes," he replied; "I've been thinking over it, an' I don't see no other way, an' it may as well be to—night as any other time."

After leaving us he was absent for about an hour. When he returned, therewere traces in his appearance of the storm through which he had passed. His hands trembled with agitation he even looked weakened as he sank into his chair.We regarded him with commiseration.

"It's over," he half whispered, "an' it was even rougher than I thought it would be. She was terrible outed, was mother. I reckon I never see her so outed before. She jest raged and tore. It was most more than I could stand, Esmeraldy," and he dropped his head upon his hands for support. "Seemed like it was the Markis as laid heaviest upon her," he proceeded. "She was terrible sot on the Markis, an' every time she think of him, she'd just rear — she'd just rear. I never stood up agen mother afore, an' I hope I sha'n't never have it to do again in my time. I'm kinder wore out."

Little by little we learned much of what had passed, though he evidently withheld the most for the sake of Mademoiselle, and it was some time before he broke the news to her that her mother's doors were closed against her.

"I think you'll find it pleasanter a—stoppin' here," he said, "if Mis' Dimar'll board ye until — until the time fur startin' home. Her sperrit was so up that she said she didn't aim to see you no more, an' you know how she is, Esmeraldy, when her sperrit's up."

Esmerelda

The girl went and clung around his neck, kneeling at his side, and shedding tears.

"Oh! father!" she cried, "you've bore a great deal for me; you've bore more than any one knows, and all for me."

He looked rather grave, as he shook his head at the fire.

"That's so, Esmeraldy," he replied; "but we allus seemed nigh to each other, somehow, and when it come to the wust, I was bound to kinder make a stand fur you, as I couldn't have made fur myself. I couldn't have done it fur myself. Lord! No!"

So Mademoiselle remained with us, and Clelie assisted her to prepare her simple outfit, and in the evening the tall young lover came into our apartment and sat looking on, which aspect of affairs, I will confess, was entirely new to Clelie, and yet did not displease her.

"Their candor moves me," she said. "He openly regards her with adoration. At parting she accompanies him to the door, and he embraces her tenderly, and yet one is not repelled. It is the love of the lost Arcadia — serious and innocent."

Finally, we went with them one morning to the American Chapel in the Rue de Berri, and they were united in our presence and that of Monsieur, who was indescribably affected.

After the completion of the ceremony, he presented Monsieur Wash with a package.

"It's papers as I've had drawd up fur Esmeraldy," he said. "It'll start you well out in the world, an' after me and mother's gone, there's no one but you and her to have the rest. The Lord — may the Lord bless ye!"

We accompanied them to Havre, and did not leave them until the last moment. Monsieur was strangely excited, and clung to the hands of his daughter and son-in-law, talking fast and nervously, and pouring out messages to be delivered to his distant friends.

"Tell 'em I'd like powerful well to see 'em all, an' I'd have come only — only things was kinder inconvenient. Sometime, perhaps — — "

Esmerelda

But here he was obliged to clear his throat, as his voice had become extremely husky. And, havin, done this, he added in an undertone:

"You see, Esmeraldy, I couldn't, because of mother, as I've swore not to go back on. Wash, he wouldn't go back on you, however high your sperrit was, an' I can't go back on mother."

The figures of the young couple standing at the side, Monsieur Wash holding his wife to his breast with one strong arm, were the last we saw as the ship moved slowly away.

"It is obscurity to which they are returning," I said, half unconsciously.

"It is love," said Clelie.

The father, who had been standing apart, came back to us, replacing in his pocket his handkerchief.

They are young an' likely, you see," said Monsieur, "an' life before them, an' it's nat'ral as she should have chose Wash, as was young too, an' sot on her. Lord, it's nat'ral, an' I wouldn't have it no otherways."

A CARCANET.

NOT what the chemists say they be,
Are pearls — they never grew;
They come not from the hollow sea,
They come from heaven in dew!

Down in the Indian sea it slips,
Through green and briny whirls,
Where great shells catch it in their lips,
And kiss it into pearls!

If dew can be so beauteous made,
Oh, why not tears, my girl?
Why not your tears? Be not afraid —
I do but kiss a pearl!

CPSIA information can be obtained at www.ICGtesting.com
Printed in the USA
BVOW09s0056040615

402975BV00025B/84/P